Take Your Victory!

Corbin N. Nash

Unless otherwise indicated, all Scripture quotations are taken from the *King James Version* of the Bible.

Take Your Victory!
ISBN 0-9649747-0-3
Copyright © 1995 by Corbin N. Nash
PO Box 58-1942
Tulsa, OK 74158-1942

Second Printing January 2001

Published by
Christian Outreach Ministries Evangelist, Inc.
PO Box 58-1942
Tulsa, OK 74158-1942

Printed in the United States of America.

All rights reserved under International Copyright Law.

Contents and/or cover may not be reproduced in whole or in part in any form without the express written consent of the Publisher.

To my mother,
Alice Nash,
and in memory of my father,
Corbin J. Nash,
who raised their children in the church.

Also to my daughter,
Cortney,
to my brother,
Broderick,
and my sisters,
Durrenda and Carmelleta.

Contents

Endorsement	i
Introduction	ii
1. The Battlefield	1
2. Whom Did God Choose?	5
3. Keep Your Testimony	9
4. Use What God Gave You	15
5. Talk Back to the Devil	21
6. The Battle	25
7. Shouting Time!	29
Prayer	31

Endorsement

"Corbin Nash has made a powerful parallel to God's choice in David and His choice in you. The winning power to slay Goliath is yours today. This book is great for any battle you are facing."

Rev. Bob Yandian
Pastor Grace Fellowship
Tulsa, Oklahoma

Introduction

One day while sitting at my desk, I began to read the story of David as recorded in First Samuel Chapter 17. While reading it, I realized that some of the same principles that are used in the New Testament were also practiced by David under the Old Covenant.

The more I read, the more I was spiritually uplifted! Therefore, I am writing this book to share these observations in the hopes that you, too, may be blessed and encouraged in the Lord.

Before we begin, we must realize that at this point in David's life, he was not the mighty warrior that we so often hear about. He was just a young man who was sent as an errand boy to bring his brothers food. He had no intention of fighting against a giant warrior. But because David walked with God, the Lord could use him to take the victory for the entire nation of Israel.

So often we forget about using biblical examples when facing our own battles, but these examples will help us win our own battles.

God gave the victory to David, and He will surely give it to us! We serve a God who never changes. He's the same God that David served, and He is waiting to help us receive the victory in every circumstance in our lives.

Today everyone wants the victory, but how are we preparing ourselves to get it? God is on our side, but we also have a part in winning our spiritual battles!

To win a victory means we are successful in a contest or struggle. Without a struggle, enemy, or antagonist there simply is no victory! But we must stand against the enemy in order to taste the sweet fruit of victory.

Engaging in battle also means that there is a possibility that we may lose the skirmish. To "lose" means *to be defeated*. It refers to *destruction*, *frustration*, or *nullification*. That's why no one wants to lose. Because of this, unsaved people in the world system have developed many strategies to win.

For example, libraries are filled with books on how to win. The subjects range from chess to baseball, and many more books are being published every day. Man has geared himself to employ any tactic to win, sometimes even to the detriment of the lives and well-being of innocent people.

As Christians, we can't use the same strategies as the world, because we can't fight dirty. Yet we are in a battle against the dirtiest fighter of all ages, Satan! He's trying to destroy us, but he has been defeated by Jesus Christ (Col. 2:15). Therefore, we *can* keep a foot on Satan's head, declaring the victory over him!

We are more than conquerors, and in God's Word, He has given us *His* strategies to win. Our fight is not a physical fight; it is a spiritual fight.

EPHESIANS 6:12
12 *For* **we wrestle not against flesh and blood, but against PRINCIPALITIES, against POWERS, against the RULERS OF THE DARKNESS OF THIS WORLD, against SPIRITUAL WICKEDNESS in high** *places.*

Jesus Christ has already defeated the devil! All principalities, powers, rulers of darkness, and spiritual wickedness in high places must come subject to you through Jesus' Name (Phil. 2:9-11).

Chapter 1
The Battlefield

Each one of us in life will experience tests, trials, and tribulations. God's Word says so (1 Peter 1:6,7). However, we never need to be defeated by them. Your victory in the spiritual battles of this life will determine your success in life.

In the Old Testament, the Israelites and Philistines also faced many battles. These two great forces had been enemies for many years. Each side had their own battle plans, and they were prepared to meet in the valley to fight! There could only be one winner, but both armies had geared up to win.

1 SAMUEL 17:1-3
1 Now the Philistines gathered together their armies to battle, and were gathered together at Shochoh, which belongeth to Judah, and pitched between Shochoh and Azekah, in Ephesdammim.

2 And Saul and the men of Israel were gathered together, and pitched by the valley of Elah, and set the battle in array against the Philistines.

3 And the Philistines stood on a mountain on the one side, and Israel stood on a mountain on the other side: and there was a valley between them.

The Bible lets us know that the Philistines had a secret weapon, a warrior by the name of Goliath.

Goliath was almost ten-feet-tall, and wore a helmet of brass. He also wore a coat of mail weighing about one hundred and eighty pounds, and his spearhead alone weighed twenty-one pounds! No one had ever been able to conquer Goliath.

Goliath was so sure of himself in battle that he presented himself before Israel for forty days seeking a person to fight him. Because of Goliath's terrifying taunts, a spirit of fear came upon Israel. The situation looked hopeless and impossible to win, but God had already prepared a warrior by the name of David to defeat this invincible giant.

The very size of Goliath was probably the reason that the experienced soldiers of Israel were afraid of Goliath. He looked mean and impossible to defeat.

Likewise, the devil will always try to make situations look impossible in our lives. He will try to disguise the complexity of a situation to get us to quit. He is always trying to make our victory seem harder than it really is so we will give up the faith fight and let him win.

But we must remember that no matter how difficult our battle looks, it is an easy task in the hands of a mighty God.

So don't look at the difficulty of the task, but look to an almighty God!

1 TIMOTHY 6:12
12 FIGHT THE GOOD FIGHT OF FAITH, lay hold on eternal life, whereunto thou art also called, and hast professed a good profession before many witnesses.

Therefore the most important fight the Christian will ever fight is the faith fight. The Christian's battlefield is not in some valley, but most often in our minds. The enemy will try to fill our thoughts with visions of defeat, and he attempts to win by intimidation.

2 CORINTHIANS 10:3-5
3 For though we walk in the flesh, we do not war after the flesh:

4 (For the weapons of our warfare *are* not carnal, but mighty through God to the pulling down of strong holds;)

5 Casting down IMAGINATIONS, and EVERY HIGH THING that exalteth itself against the knowledge of God, and bringing into captivity every THOUGHT to the obedience of Christ.

Paul is saying here that our weapons are not fleshy, but spiritual. Not only are they spiritual, but they are mighty. They are powerful and effective against our enemy.

Paul goes on to say that we must cast down negative thoughts or imaginations so that we can have the mind of Christ. Philippians 2:5 reads, "Let this mind be in you, which was also in Christ Jesus."

That's why the Word tells you to renew your mind so you can have God's perspective on your situation.

ROMANS 12:2
2 And be not conformed to this world: but be ye TRANSFORMED BY THE RENEWING OF YOUR MIND, that ye may prove what *is* that good, and acceptable, and perfect, will of God.

But you won't be able to have the mind of Christ unless you study, meditate on, and believe God's Word. With our minds focused on the things of God, we begin to have a God-focus on our situations, and our problems begin to look small. We know that with men, many things are impossible, but with God *all* things are possible.

Mark 10:27
27 And Jesus looking upon them saith, With men it is impossible, but not with God: for with God all things are possible.

There is no defeat in God. He is waiting for an opportunity to show Himself strong in our lives. He wants us to look to Him for the answers to our problems. When things look impossible, God is with us to make us successful.

If you want to know what God thinks concerning your situation, look first to His Word. In His Word is the power to transform any person, any situation, any problem — including *you!*

Chapter 2
Whom Did God Choose?

In the midst of battle, David appears. At this point in his life he was just a young man, not the king that we read about later. David was sent to the battleground not to fight, but to take provisions to his brothers. While on the battleground, David heard Goliath boasting.

1 SAMUEL 17:8-11
8 And he [Goliath] **stood and cried unto the armies of Israel, and said unto them, Why are ye come out to set your battle in array? am not I a Philistine, and ye servants to Saul? choose you a man for you, and let him come down to me.**

9 If he be able to fight with me, and to kill me, then will we be your servants: but if I prevail against him, and kill him, then shall ye be our servants, and serve us.

10 And the Philistine said, I defy the armies of Israel this day; give me a man, that we may fight together.

11 When Saul and all Israel heard those words of the Philistine, they were dismayed, and greatly afraid.

We see that Goliath's boasting made Israel fearful, but this was not the case with David. He did not react in fear.

1 SAMUEL 17:23
23 And as he [David] **talked with them** [his brothers]**, behold, there came up the champion, the Philistine of Gath, Goliath**

by name, out of the armies of the Philistines, and spake according to the same words: and David heard them.

David did not respond in fear as did Saul and the armies of Israel. His response was much different. David saw that Goliath was really defying God and that made David furious. He was upset that Goliath had the nerve to come against God's chosen people.

1 SAMUEL 17:26
26 And David spake to the men that stood by him, saying, What shall be done to the man that killeth this Philistine, and taketh away the reproach from Israel? for who *is* **this uncircumcised Philistine, that he should defy the armies of the living God?**

Our response should be the same when we see the devil in operation. We should get angry at Satan, too, and bind his strategy against us (Matt. 18:18).

We need to take a stand against Satan! And if the enemy is in our house with sickness, disease, strife, or poverty, let's kick him out. Life is too short to tolerate his presence in our lives. The Bible says to "Submit yourselves therefore to God. RESIST THE DEVIL, and he will flee from you" (James 4:7).

Therefore, be sure you are not giving the devil access to you through any open door of disobedience or sin. Submit yourself to God and His Word, and close the door on the devil in your life!

Out of all the Israelites, there was no one but David prepared to fight the enemy. David was not about to let Goliath defy the Most High God! He decided to accept the challenge!

1 SAMUEL 17:32
32 And David said to Saul, Let no man's heart fail because of him; thy servant will go and fight with this Philistine.

Likewise, there are times in our spiritual walk when we must take up the challenge too. Never let Satan defeat you!

There are certain times in our lives when God allows us to walk through certain valleys. There are certain trials that we are permitted to go through so that we can grow in the things of God. When we were babies in the Lord, God allowed other Christians to pray for us and hold our hands while we were going through tests and trails.

But the day is coming when *you* are the only one who can take your victory. The victory is yours, but the battle is the Lord's. First Samuel 17:47 says that the battle is the Lord's, and He will give the enemy into our hands.

God wants us to go into the battle knowing that He will give us the victory. The Bible also says, ". . . Be not afraid nor dismayed by reason of this great multitude; for the battle is not yours, but God's" (2 Chron. 20:15).

David was God's chosen warrior to win the battle, and so are you. Don't worry. With the Word of God in your heart and mouth, you can stand victoriously against the wiles of the devil.

As long as you remember that God has chosen you and that He has already defeated the devil, you'll win every time. You must continue to tell yourself that the battle has already been won by Jesus.

Many of us do not operate in that reality. If we did, we'd know that trials and tribulations are opportunities for our development, not our demise. God has chosen us to succeed, not to fail.

Chapter 3
Keep Your Testimony

King Saul did not think David was able to fight Goliath. He looked at David and realized that he was only a young man. Saul probably considered the fact that David was not trained in Israel as a soldier and therefore was not qualified to fight.

David did not see it that way because he did not look at himself, but he looked to God. He remembered what God had done for him in the past, and he was confident that God would do it again.

1 SAMUEL 17:33-37
33 And Saul said to David, Thou art not able to go against this Philistine to fight with him: for thou art but a youth, and he a man of war from his youth.

34 And David said unto Saul, Thy servant kept his father's sheep, and there came a lion, and a bear, and took a lamb out of the flock:

35 And I went out after him, and smote him, and delivered it out of his mouth: and when he arose against me, I caught him by his beard, and smote him, and slew him.

36 Thy servant slew both the lion and the bear: and this uncircumcised Philistine shall be as one of them, seeing he hath defied the armies of the living God.

37 David said moreover, The Lord that delivered me out of the paw of the lion, and out of the paw of the bear, HE WILL

DELIVER ME OUT OF THE HAND OF THIS PHILISTINE. And Saul said unto David, Go, and the Lord be with thee.

David kept his testimony! Even when confronted with a mighty giant, David didn't talk about the problem; he testified about what God would do for him!

If we are to be victors, we must never forget what our God has done for us. Remembering what God has done for us in the past will help us gear up for the spiritual battles in the future.

Recount your testimonies! Begin to talk about them! Rehearse your victories in God!

When we talk about the problem, we begin to worry. Many of us have a tendency to worry anyway. We worry about the future. We worry about the present. We worry, worry, worry. When we talk, we must testify about the greatness of God, *not* about our problems.

Besides, why worry? Hasn't God delivered you from your troubles in the past? You should have David's attitude. David's attitude was this: If God delivered me in the past, He will deliver me in the future!

We don't need to worry; we just need to let our request be made known to God. The Bible says, "Be careful for nothing; but in every thing by prayer and supplication with thanksgiving let your requests be made known unto God" (Phil. 4:6).

Worry is not what gave the victory to the Christians in the Book of Revelation. It was their testimonies. Revelation 12:11 says, "And they overcame him by the blood of the Lamb, and by the word of their TESTIMONY. . . ." Yes, we can overcome the devil with the word of our testimony by recounting the great things God has done for us.

Personal testimonies are not the Christians only defense against the wiles of the devil. We must also lay hold of what the Word says about us. God's Word has the power to defeat the devil (Jer. 23:29).

During the ministry of Jesus, we can see that He spoke what God's Word said about Him so He could stand strong against those who came against Him. What God said about Jesus was found in the Book of Isaiah. Jesus quoted from Isaiah 61 in this passage in Luke.

LUKE 4:17-21
17 And there was delivered unto him [Jesus] the book of the prophet Esaias [Isaiah]. And when he had opened the book, he found the place where it was written,

18 The Spirit of the Lord *is* **upon me, because he hath anointed me to preach the gospel to the poor; he hath sent me to heal the brokenhearted, to preach deliverance to the captives, and recovering of sight to the blind, to set at liberty them that are bruised,**

19 To preach the acceptable year of the Lord.

20 And he closed the book, and he gave *it* **again to the minister, and sat down. And the eyes of all them that were in the synagogue were fastened on him.**

21 And he began to say unto them, This day is this scripture fulfilled in your ears.

Jesus made the religious hypocrites mad when He spoke what God's Word said about Him. Likewise, we upset the enemy when we speak what God says about us. Why? Because there is power in God's Word. We are mightily testifying about God's greatness when we speak God's Word over us.

ISAIAH 55:11
11 So shall my word [God's Word] **be that goeth forth out of my mouth: it shall not return unto me void, but it shall accomplish that which I** [God] **please, and it shall prosper in the thing whereto I sent it.**

Think about it. If we speak God's Word, it can't return void! That's why the devil gets mad when we use the Word. He can't stand against It. He's tried for ages to stand against God's Word, but he can't. The Word of God endures forever and will never pass away (Matt. 24:35).

I remember a time when I was out of a job. Several months had passed, and I had no solid leads. Bills had to be paid, and financial obligations were due, but I resisted the devil's attempt to make me worry.

From deep within came another source of testimony — the testimony of God's Word. The Bible says, ". . . When the enemy shall come in like a flood, the Spirit of the Lord shall lift up a standard against him" (Isa. 59:19). The Spirit and the Word comforted me during this time. Victory came as the Word of God begin to change my circumstances.

Here are some of the Scriptures that the Lord gave me during my time of need:

ISAIAH 54:17
17 No weapon that is formed against thee shall prosper; and every tongue *that* **shall rise against thee in judgment thou shalt condemn.**

1 JOHN 4:4
4 Ye are of God, little children, and have overcome them: because greater is he that is in you, than he that is in the world.

PHILIPPIANS 4:19
19 But my God shall supply all my need according to his riches in glory by Christ Jesus.

Yes, God's Word is our testimony. Everything that the Word says about us is true. The Word of God has the power to make our circumstances conform to God's will for our lives!

That's why we must get into the Word and claim God's promises. We must know who we are in Christ!

We must know that God has given us all things that pertain to life and godliness (2 Peter 1:3). If the Word says it, I believe it, and that settles it!

Chapter 4
Use What God Gave You

Even though King Saul gave David permission to fight Goliath, Saul still did not believe that David was properly equipped for battle. Saul tried to equip David with his own armor by putting a helmet of brass upon David's head and arming him with a coat of mail.

David's response was interesting. He did not want to wear Saul's armor into battle because he was used to fighting the Lord's way, not man's way. He was used to fighting with the Lord as his defense.

1 SAMUEL 17:38-40
38 And Saul armed David with his armour, and he put an helmet of brass upon his head; also he armed him with a coat of mail.

39 And David girded his sword upon his armour, and he assayed to go; for he had not proved it. And David said unto Saul, I cannot go with these; for I have not proved them. And David put them off him.

40 And he took his staff in his hand, and chose him five smooth stones out of the brook, and put them in a shepherd's bag which he had, even in a scrip; and his sling was in his hand: and he drew near to the Philistine.

David had grown accustomed to using his sling, and he trusted it more than he did the armor of a king.

He knew the Lord was his defense, not a suit of armor.

This is a good example for you in your time of need! You need to trust that God will bring out your God-given abilities that He has put within you to get the job done (1 Peter 4:11). When you are in a tribulation, trust that God has well-equipped you to come out victoriously.

There are too many people nowadays who are trying to be something they are not. If God has equipped them to use a sling, they shouldn't try to use a sword! There are too many people trying to use a sword when the sling is really more their kind of weapon.

For example, I've seen many cases in the church where people are trying to hold a position that a person called them to — not God.

If you are called to the fivefold ministry, go for it, but please do not enter a ministry God has not called you to.

It's very important to identify your gifts and callings and stay within them. They will be developed as you serve the Lord (Phil. 2:13).

The Book of Matthew speaks about the parable of the talents. There is much to learn in these verses about using your gifts and callings for God:

Use What God Gave You 17

MATTHEW 25:14-30
14 For the kingdom of heaven is as a man travelling into a far country, who called his own servants, and delivered unto them his goods.

15 And unto one he gave five talents, to another two, and to another one; to every man according to his several ability; and straightway took his journey.

16 Then he that had received the five talents went and traded with the same, and made them other five talents.

17 And likewise he that had received two, he also gained other two.

18 But he that had received one went and digged in the earth, and hid his lord's money.

19 After a long time the Lord of those servants cometh, and reckoneth with them.

20 And so he that had received five talents, saying, Lord, thou deliveredst unto me five talents: behold, I have gained beside them five talents more.

21 His Lord said unto him, Well done, thou good and faithful servant: thou hast been faithful over a few things, I will make thee ruler over many things: enter thou into the joy of thy lord.

22 He also that had received two talents came and said, Lord, thou deliveredst unto me two talents: behold, I have gained two other talents besides them.

23 His lord said unto him, Well done, good and faithful servant; thou hast been faithful over a few things, I will

make thee ruler over many things: enter thou into the joy of thy lord.

24 Then he which had received the one talent came and said, Lord, I knew thee that thou art an hard man, reaping where thou hast not sown, and gathering where thou hast not strawed:

25 And I was afraid, and went and hid thy talent in the earth: lo, there thou hast that is thine.

26 His lord answered and said unto him, Thou wicked and slothful servant, thou knewest that I reap where I sowed not, and gather where I have not strawed:

27 Thou oughtest therefore to have put my money to the exchangers, and then at my coming I should have received mine own usury.

28 Take therefore the talent from him, and give it unto him which hath ten talents.

29 For unto every one that hath shall be given, and he shall have abundance: but from him that hath not shall be taken away even that which he hath.

30 And cast ye the unprofitable servant into outer darkness: there shall be weeping and gnashing of teeth.

The master gave each of his servants talents to invest. The "talents" in this parable were monies, not gifts or personal endowments.

One servant was given five talents, another two, and another one. When the master returned from his journey, he inquired how each servant had done with his talents.

The first two servants had traded them and gained even more. The master's response was, "Well done, thou good and faithful servant: thou hast been faithful over a few things, I will make thee ruler over many things..." (v. 23).

In the other case, the servant with only one talent did not gain any more talents. He hid his talent because he feared losing it. His master was not pleased. He said, "Thou wicked and slothful servant, thou knewest that I reap where I sowed not, and gather where I have not strawed..." (v. 26).

Let's apply this parable to our Christian walk. I believe that God has given every Christian gifts and graces, and He will hold us responsible for how we have used what He has given us: "... For unto whomsoever much is given, of him shall be much required..." (Luke 12:48).

Notice that the first two servants were given a different number of talents, but both were rewarded for developing their talents. The Lord is showing us in this parable that the size of the talent is not important. But how we develop what God has given us *is* important.

Are you developing your talents? Your gifts are important! How are you using what God gave you?

Chapter 5
Talk Back to the Devil

In the boxing world, there is usually a lot of talking before a fight. Both opponents talk about each other to promote the fight and to intimidate each other.

David's battle with Goliath was no exception. As David drew near, the Philistine giant begin to boast. Goliath tried to intimidate David.

The Bible says ". . . the tongue is a little member, and boasteth great things. Behold, how great a matter a little fire kindleth" (James 3:5). Goliath used his words as a weapon against David to frighten this young Israelite!

1 SAMUEL 17:43,44
43 And the Philistine said unto David, *Am* **I a dog, that thou comest to me with staves? And the Philistine cursed David by his gods.**

44 And the Philistine said to David, Come to me, and I will give thy flesh unto the fowls of the air, and to the beasts of the field.

These were boastful words, but David did not let the enemy's words intimidate him. He spoke back to his enemy.

1 SAMUEL 17:45,46
45 Then said David to the Philistine, Thou comest to me with a sword, and with a spear, and with a shield: but I come to thee in the name of the Lord of hosts, the God of the armies of Israel, whom thou hast defied.

46 This day will the Lord deliver thee into mine hand; and I will smite thee and take thine head from thee; and I will give the carcases of the host of the Philistines this day unto the fowls of the air, and to the wild beasts of the earth; that all the earth may know that there is a God in Israel.

David talked back to Goliath! He didn't just give in to him. David told this Philistine giant that he would be defeated — not in David's name, but in the Name of the Lord of hosts.

So often we forget that we have authority over the devil. We should be ready to talk back to him using the Word of God as our defense. Jesus did just that. Every time the devil would try to tempt Him, Jesus would quote the Word to Satan.

Jesus overcame the devil with the Word of God. When Satan came to tempt Jesus, the Lord defeated him every single time by saying, "It is written."

The devil tried to make Jesus turn the stones to bread, but Jesus said, "It is written, Man shall not live by bread alone, but by every word that proceedeth out of the mouth of God" (Matt. 4:4).

The devil tried to make Jesus jump from the pinnacle of the temple. Jesus answered and said, "It is written again, Thou shalt not tempt the Lord thy God" (Matt. 4:7).

Again the devil came to Jesus and offered Him all the kingdoms of the world. Jesus finally said, "Get thee hence, Satan: for it is written, Thou shalt worship the Lord thy God, and him only shalt thou serve" (Matt. 4:1-11).

For every temptation, Jesus responded with the Word of God. If God's Word is in us, we can put the devil on the run. God's Word has power and authority over the devil and his strategies. The Word is a potent power against the devil.

The Bible teaches us that we have authority in Jesus' Name. Mark 16:17 says, "And these signs shall follow them that believe; In my name shall they cast out devils. . . ." Armed with the Name of Jesus, we can talk back to the devil and put him in his place!

Chapter 6
The Battle

David approached the enemy, but not before he applied certain faith principles. Although this story was written in the Old Testament, New Testament principles were in operation. These are the principles that David used to defeat the devil:

1. *Keep Your Testimony :*

   David had a testimony. He remembered what God had done for him in the past and he knew that God would not fail him now. David spoke boldly about the victories God had won for him.

2. *Use What God Gave You* :

   David did not use the King's armor, but he trusted God to give him the victory with the weapon God had given him, a sling.

3. *Talk Back to the Devil* :

   David refused to be intimidated by the words of his enemy. David talked back to the devil and put him in his place!

If we apply the proper scriptural principles, the devil will lose every time! We must realize that Satan was defeated at the Cross, and the victory is ours.

David knew that his victory belonged to God, and it was his faith in God that allowed him to claim the victory.

1 SAMUEL 17:47-49
47 And all this assembly shall know that the Lord saveth not with sword and spear: for THE BATTLE IS THE LORD'S, and he will give you into our hands.

48 And it came to pass, when the Philistine arose, and came and drew nigh to meet David, that David hasted, and ran toward the army to meet the Philistine.

49 And David put his hand in his bag, and took thence a stone, and slang it, and smote the Philistine in his forehead, that the stone sunk into his forehead; and he fell upon his face to the earth.

David took his victory with a sling and one rock! What looks weak in the eyes of man is strong in the hand of God! Once David fulfilled his part and released that stone in faith, God did His part.

As David released that sling, I would not be shocked to learn that God commanded the angels to direct the path and the speed of that rock!

In any case, the Bible tells us that the rock hit the Philistine giant with so much force that it sunk into his forehead and killed him. With one rock, David defeated his enemy!

God has the same plan for us. Only our rock is the Lord Jesus Christ. We are standing on a rock. Jesus said, ". . . and upon this ROCK I will build my church. . . ." (Matt.16:18).

As Christians, we are part of the Church and we stand on the Rock, the Lord Jesus Christ. Peter referred to Christ when he said, "To whom coming, as unto a LIVING STONE, disallowed indeed of men, but chosen of God, and precious" (1 Peter 2:4).

Our rock is Jesus! He died to give us victory in every situation, and the devil has no place in our lives. God's plan in the beginning was to bruise the head of the devil (Gen. 3:15).

That was a symbol of the fact that the Lord Jesus Christ would defeat the devil and deprive him of his power (Col. 2:15). God defeated the devil for us with His Rock, and that Rock was Jesus Christ!

If we believe in God's Word and use Bible principles, we can also receive the victory every single time!

You may think that your problem is unique or too difficult for God, but I am a witness to the fact that God can make a way when there is no way. There is no problem that God can't solve. You just need to trust Him. The battle is not yours, but it belongs to the Lord (2 Chron. 20:17).

Chapter 7
Shouting Time!

David not only killed his enemy, but he ended up with his enemy's sword! This shows that God will use the weapons the enemy tries to form against you to bless you.

For example, is your boss using his position at the office to harm you? Don't worry about it. Take it to God in prayer, and God may give you his position!

1 SAMUEL 17:50,51
50 So David prevailed over the Philistine with a sling and with a stone, and smote the Philistine, and slew him; but there was no sword in the hand of David.

51 Therefore David ran, and stood upon the Philistine, and took his sword, and drew it out of the sheath thereof, and slew him, and cut off his head therewith. And when the Philistines saw their champion was dead, they fled.

David not only killed the Philistine with a rock, but he used his opponent's sword to take off his head. Remember, earlier David stated that he would do just that, ". . . I will smite thee, and take thine HEAD from thee . . . " (1 Sam.17:46).

When David received the victory, the men of Israel shouted and pursued the entire Philistine army. There was great joy in the valley because of the

Israelite's victory. David's triumph encouraged the rest of the men to pursue the enemy too. David did not have the respect of the other warriors until after he received his victory.

I believe that this is the same thing that happens to us. When we are successful, this encourages other Christians. Our battle and victory may be a motivating force for someone else to receive his victory.

On the other hand, don't expect everyone to sympathize with you while you are on the battlefield. Get the victory first, and then they will rejoice to hear your testimony.

I remember the testimony services we used to have in my hometown church. On occasion I would come to church feeling down because I was facing a problem. But as I listened to others testify, I was encouraged by their testimonies.

There was something else I enjoyed about those services. Everyone rejoiced when they heard about another conquest over the enemy.

You see, your victory is important. It will not only bless you, it will also bless others. Remember God is in the blessing business, and He loves you and wants to bless you!

So take your VICTORY!

Prayer

Many of us would like the victory in our lives but are not able to obtain it simply because we are not in the Body of Christ — we have never been saved.

This is easy as asking the Lord to come into your heart to be your Lord and Savior. Realize that Jesus died for your sins. If you have not accepted Jesus, please repeat the following prayer:

Dear God, Your Word says that You so loved the world that You gave Your only begotten Son, so that whoever believes in Him will have eternal life (John 3:16).

I accept Your Word and ask You to forgive my sins based on the death, burial, and resurrection of Jesus.

Jesus, please come into my heart. Be my Lord and Savior and save me from my sins. Beginning this day I will serve only You.

Thank You for saving me! I now have the victory!

To order books and tapes by Corbin N. Nash,
or to contact him for speaking engagements,
please write:

Christian Outreach Ministries Evangelist
P. O. Box 58-1942
Tulsa, OK 74158-1942

or call :
1-918-496-1087